BLANCHESTER PUBLIC LIBRARY
110 N BROADWAY
BLANCHESTER OH 45107

11/28/2005 $22.78   ~~BLANCHESTER~~ BY THE ~~BLANCHESTER PUB~~ .IC LIBRARY

W9-CLV-971

BLANCHESTER PUBLIC LIBRARY
110 N. BROADWAY
BLANCHESTER, OHIO 45107

Native Americans

Wampanoag

Barbara A. Gray-Kanatiiosh

ABDO Publishing Company

visit us at
www.abdopub.com

Published by ABDO Publishing Company, 4940 Viking Drive, Suite 622, Edina, Minnesota 55435. Copyright © 2004 by Abdo Consulting Group, Inc. International copyrights reserved in all countries. No part of this book may be reproduced in any form without written permission from the publisher.

Printed in the United States.

Cover Photo: Stephen Nacci
Interior Photos: AP/Wide World pp. 28, 29, 30; Corbis p. 4
Illustrations: David Kanietakeron Fadden pp. 7, 9, 11, 13, 15, 17, 19, 21, 23, 25, 27
Editors: Kate A. Conley, Jennifer R. Krueger, Kristin Van Cleaf
Art Direction & Maps: Neil Klinepier

Library of Congress Cataloging-in-Publication Data

Gray-Kanatiiosh, Barbara A., 1963-
      Wampanoag / Barbara A. Gray-Kanatiiosh.
        p. cm. -- (Native Americans)
      Includes bibliographical references and index.
      Summary: An introduction to the history, social structure, customs, and present life of the Wampanoag Indians.
      ISBN 1-57765-941-4
      1. Wampanoag Indians--History--Juvenile literature. 2. Wampanoag Indians--Social life and customs--Juvenile
literature. [1.Wampanoag Indians. 2. Indians of North America--New England.] I. Title. II. Native Americans
(Edina, Minn.)

E99.W2G73 2003
974.4004'973--dc21
                                                                              2003040339

About the Author: Barbara A. Gray-Kanatiiosh, JD
Barbara Gray-Kanatiiosh, JD, Ph.D. ABD, is an Akwesasne Mohawk. She resides at the Mohawk Nation and is of the Wolf Clan. She has a Juris Doctorate from Arizona State University, where she was one of the first recipients of ASU's special certificate in Indian Law. Barbara's Ph.D. is in Justice Studies at ASU. She is currently working on her dissertation, which concerns the impacts of environmental injustice on indigenous culture. Barbara works hard to educate children about Native Americans through her writing and Web site, where children may ask questions and receive a written response about the Haudenosaunee culture. The Web site is: www.peace4turtleisland.org

About the Illustrator: David Kanietakeron Fadden
David Kanietakeron Fadden is a member of the Akwesasne Mohawk Wolf Clan. His work has appeared in publications such as *Akwesasne Notes, Indian Time,* and the *Northeast Indian Quarterly.* Examples of his work have also appeared in various publications of the Six Nations Indian Museum in Onchiota, NY. His work has also appeared in "How the West Was Lost: Always the Enemy," produced by Gannett Production, which appeared on the Discovery Channel. David's work has been exhibited in Albany, NY; the Lake Placid Center for the Arts; Centre Strathearn in Montreal, Quebec; North Country Community College in Saranac Lake, NY; Paul Smith's College in Paul Smiths, NY; and at the Unison Arts & Learning Center in New Paltz, NY.

Contents

Where They Lived 4

Society 6

Food 8

Homes 10

Clothing 12

Crafts 14

Family 16

Children 18

Myths 20

War 22

Contact with Europeans 24

Metacom 26

The Wampanoag Today 28

Glossary 31

Web Sites 31

Index 32

Where They Lived

The multicolored Aquinnah Cliffs are sacred to the Wampanoag.

The Wampanoag (WOM-puh-NO-ag) lived on the eastern coast of North America. Because of where they lived, the Wampanoag were one of the first peoples to see the sun rise in the east every morning. In fact, the name *Wampanoag* means "People of the First Light," or "People of the Dawn." The people spoke Wampanoag, a language in the Algonquian language family.

The Wampanoag homelands stretched from east of Narragansett Bay to the Atlantic Ocean. The lands included what is now eastern Rhode Island and southern Massachusetts. The islands of Nantucket and Martha's Vineyard were also Wampanoag lands. Their neighbors included the Nipmuc, Narraganset, Massachuset, and Pequot tribes.

Glaciers had provided the Wampanoag homelands with clay deposits, boulders, ponds, lakes, rivers, and bays. The inland was forested with oak, maple, beech, and birch trees. Evergreens such as white pine, spruce, and hemlock also grew there. The shores held marshes, dunes, and sandy shorelines. The islands were combinations of shorelines, hills, marshes, and wooded areas.

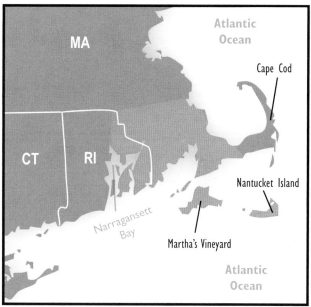

Wampanoag Homelands

Society

Wampanoag society was very close. The people depended on one another for survival. They lived together in many villages. Together, the communities formed a **confederacy** led by a grand **sachem**.

Each village had its own chief, subchief, and Council of Elders. These chiefs were elected by the people. A chief did not lead by ruling the people, but by **consensus**. The entire village met with the chiefs and Council of Elders to debate and come to decisions.

Besides making decisions, the Council of Elders also gave advice and kept the history of the people. The people often met with the elders to learn about Wampanoag traditions and to hear stories.

Wampanoag religious leaders were called powwaws. *Powwaws* offered prayers, conducted **rituals** in sweat lodges, and led spiritual ceremonies. Some people say that the word *powwow* came from the word *powwaw*.

The Wampanoag also held seasonal ceremonies. These ceremonies gave thanks for many things. For example, ceremonies gave thanks to the fish, the animals, the ripening berries, medicinal plants, green corn, a good harvest, and much more. During these ceremonies, the community came together to sing songs, dance, and eat.

Wampanoag chiefs led by discussing issues with the tribe and giving advice.

Food

The land and water provided food for the Wampanoag. They hunted, fished, gathered, and gardened. Hunting, fishing, and gathering were done both inland and along the shore. Each village had a well-defined territory for hunting and fishing.

Wampanoag men traveled inland to the forests to hunt for deer, elks, bears, and moose. Along the coast they hunted for smaller **game** such as rabbits, ducks, and geese. They hunted with bows and arrows, snares, and nets.

The men fished for many types of fish and shellfish. They fished in freshwater ponds, streams, and lakes for brook trout, pickerel, shad, herring, and sunfish. In the saltwater bays of the Atlantic Ocean they fished for flounder, cod, and lobsters. They also dug for clams and gathered oysters.

The Wampanoag gardens contained white flint corn, beans, squashes, and pumpkins. These gardens were planted using a method called hill planting. In this method, the Wampanoag

**Clams were a main part
of the Wampanoag's diet.**

planted corn at the top of a mound of soil. When the corn had grown a little, the people planted beans around it. Then, they planted squashes around the beans and corn. When these crops are planted together, they help each other grow.

Besides gardening, women also gathered food. In June, women took a basket and gathered wild berries. In the fall, they gathered acorns and other nuts. They also gathered cranberries from the sandy marshland bogs.

The people ate these foods in season, while they were still fresh. However, they sometimes preserved meat, fish, berries, and vegetables by drying them in the sun. The Wampanoag then stored the dried food in bark containers and saved it to eat during the winter.

Homes

Wampanoag homes were dome-shaped wigwams. They called this style of home a *wetu* (WE-too). Building a *wetu* took the skills of both men and women. The men built the frame, and the women covered it.

The Wampanoag men began by cutting down young trees to use for the frame. Next, the men dug a circular pit about 12 inches (30 cm) deep in the ground. The pit was the floor of the *wetu*. The men then bent sapling poles over the pit. They tied the poles together with rope made from plant fibers. This formed a dome.

After men built the frame, Wampanoag women wove mats to cover it. They wove the mats with cattail reeds. Women also used a combination of materials, such as bark or animal skins, to make mats.

When covering the frame, the Wampanoag left a hole open in the roof. The hole allowed smoke from the fire pit to escape. The *wetu* also had a door covered by a long cattail mat. The people slept on cattail-reed mats and animal furs.

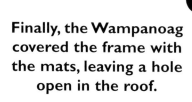

To make a *wetu*, men first cut trees and set up the trunks to make the frame.

Then, the women wove reeds and bark into mats that would be the walls and roof of the *wetu*.

Finally, the Wampanoag covered the frame with the mats, leaving a hole open in the roof.

11

Clothing

The Wampanoag felt a kinship with their natural environment. They believed it was important to use every part of the animals that they had hunted. So, the people made their clothing from animal hides and furs.

Deerskin was used to make leather. Often, the Wampanoag carved sewing needles from a deer's shinbone. Deer **sinew** was even used to make thread.

Women wore dresses made from either deerskin or elk hide. Usually, a woman's dress was one piece of animal skin with fringes on the bottom. Men wore deerskin **breechcloths** and waist-high **leggings**. Sometimes they wore a deerskin shirt, or stretched a hide across one shoulder and tied it at the waist.

The Wampanoag wore sashes across the chest or as a belt. The people finger wove these sashes from plant fibers. Both men and women wore moccasins. They commonly used deer and elk leather to make these moccasins. They sometimes used moose hide, too.

12

In cold weather, the Wampanoag wore fur robes. A fur robe was worn with the fur side touching the skin. This kept the person warm.

The people also made shell beads and jewelry. So, they sometimes wore shell necklaces. Sometimes the Wampanoag drilled holes in shells and sewed them onto their clothing.

A man and woman wearing traditional Wampanoag clothing

Crafts

The Wampanoag created many practical and decorative objects. They used most of these objects in daily life. Sometimes the people decorated the objects with shells, feathers, or paint.

Men carved cups, bowls, and ladles with stone and antler tools. These items were beautifully made. The Wampanoag considered a **burl** cup or bowl a prized possession.

The people often gathered clay from local streambeds and riverbeds. They fashioned the clay into pipes. These pipes were one piece, with a bowl and stem. Often, the Wampanoag decorated the bowl's edge with **geometric** designs.

The Wampanoag also used clay to create large pots. Once **fired**, a clay pot could be hung over a fire and used for cooking. The people often made stews, soups, and chowders in these giant pots.

The Wampanoag also gathered a special multicolored clay. They molded this clay into beautiful bowls, vases, and pots. Today, the Wampanoag still make vessels from the clay. Some use a potter's wheel, but others use the traditional **coil method**.

A Wampanoag man carefully carves a wooden bowl.

Family

Each village in the Wampanoag community was like one extended family. Survival of the Wampanoag depended on each member of the family contributing in some way. Men and women contributed equally, even though they had different jobs.

Men hunted and fished. When not out hunting and fishing, they made or repaired tools and weapons. They created the tools from wood, antler, bone, and stone. They crafted knives, bows and arrows, axes, and chisels.

The men also grew tobacco. Indian tobacco is a medium-sized plant with small yellow flowers. The Wampanoag smoked this tobacco in pipes and offered it in ceremonies to give thanks.

Wampanoag women planted and tended the other gardens. Women used hoes to control weeds and to prepare the soil for planting. This tool was a long piece of wood attached to a clamshell or deer bone.

An elder teaches Wampanoag villagers by telling them a story.

During the harvest, women wore pack baskets to help them carry crops such as corn, squashes, cranberries, and nuts. The women prepared the meats, fish, shellfish, vegetables, berries, and nuts for eating. They made sure to dry enough food for the winter.

Wampanoag elders also had special responsibilities in their families. They recounted history or told stories that taught **cultural** lessons. Winter story time was a great time for the family to come together.

Children

Wampanoag children played many games. For example, they often played running and ball games. However, the children also helped with daily village chores.

Some chores were fun, such as gathering clams. To find some types of clams, the children looked for airholes in the sand. Once they found the clams, the children dug them out from beneath the sand with a stick or large shell.

Wampanoag children gathered quahog (KOH-hawg) clams in the water. Older children waded into the water and felt in the mud with their feet. When a child found a clam, he or she could reach down to scoop it up. The people cooked the quahog clams to make a delicious clam chowder.

Boys learned to make fishing spears and traps. They learned how to fish and where to set traps to catch lobsters and crabs.

Boys also helped the men set up wooden fences. They set up these fences in a way that drove deer and small **game** to where hunters were waiting.

Wampanoag girls helped care for the younger children. They helped make clothing and prepare food. Girls also learned how to hill plant. Learning these skills helped prepare them for adulthood.

Wampanoag women sewing clothes

Myths

The Wampanoag told many stories about Moshup. He and his wife, Squant, were giants who lived a long time ago. Moshup was a man of peace and great wisdom. He loved to sit on a big rock and think. Some people say that his rock seat can still be found in Wampanoag territory.

Moshup loved whale meat. He would wade into the ocean and catch whales with one hand. His wife would pull large trees from the ground and use them to start a fire. Then, Moshup would cook the whale by holding it by its tail over the fire.

Moshup shared his whale meat with the Wampanoag. He also taught them how to hunt for whales. In thanks, the Wampanoag gave Moshup all the tobacco they had grown for a season.

Moshup took out a giant pipe and smoked the tobacco. When he was finished, Moshup emptied his pipe into the waters. The tobacco created the islands in Wampanoag territory.

Others say that Moshup dragged his toe across the land. The mark left by his toe filled with water, separating a piece of land from the mainland. This formed the island known as Martha's Vineyard.

Moshup reaches down to catch a whale for his supper.

War

The Wampanoag were a peace-loving people who did not go to war often. But, sometimes fighting became necessary to protect their hunting and fishing territories. However, the fighting did not always end in death. Sometimes the Wampanoag just harassed trespassers until they left.

When the Wampanoag did go to war, they fought with many of the same weapons they used to hunt. In close combat, the Wampanoag fought with war clubs and knives. The knives were usually made from quartz, flint, or bone.

For more distant fighting, the Wampanoag fought with bows and arrows. They chose the wood for the bow carefully. They twisted plant fibers to create the bowstring. The arrows had stone or bone tips.

Wampanoag Weapons

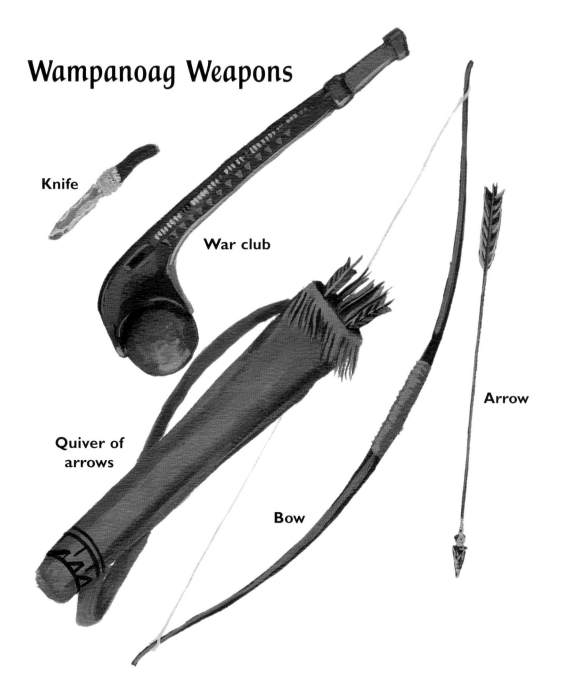

Knife

War club

Quiver of arrows

Bow

Arrow

Contact with Europeans

The Wampanoag first met Europeans around 1600. But, trading and fishing vessels had been sailing to Wampanoag shores since the 1500s. Captains often made money by capturing native people and selling them as slaves.

In the early 1600s, Squanto, a man of the Patuxet tribe, was captured and sold as a slave in Spain. He eventually escaped to England, where he learned to speak English. A few years later he returned to his homeland. Sadly, he found that most of his people had died in an **epidemic**. He joined a group of Wampanoag living nearby.

In 1620, the Pilgrims arrived in Wampanoag territory. The Pilgrims were settlers from England. They were not equipped to survive, and many died that winter. In 1621, Squanto and Massasoit, grand **sachem** of the Wampanoag, were some of the first native people to meet the Pilgrims. The two groups made a treaty that lasted a number of years.

Because Squanto spoke English, he joined the Pilgrims at Plymouth to act as an interpreter. He and the Wampanoag were generous. They taught the Pilgrims how to hill plant, how to build fishing traps, and where to hunt and fish.

The colonists and Wampanoag were friendly at first. But, tensions increased as more colonists arrived. The colonists wanted more land. They also let their livestock wander. Soon, cows and pigs were destroying Wampanoag gardens.

In addition, the Wampanoag had no **immunity** to common European diseases. For this reason, many died from the diseases brought over by the Europeans.

Wampanoag men greet a Pilgrim settler.

Metacom

Metacom was a famous Wampanoag chief who was born around 1640. The English called him King Philip. The English called him king because they mistakenly thought native leaders ruled the way kings did in England.

Metacom was the son of Chief Massasoit. He grew up watching his father help the Pilgrims survive in the New World. Massasoit was a generous leader. He gave the Pilgrims land and showed them how to grow food. Massasoit died in 1661. His first son, Wamsutta, then became chief. But, Wamsutta died a year later. Metacom became chief in 1662.

By this time, problems had developed between European settlers and the native tribes. For example, the English wanted more Wampanoag land for settlement. However, land was owned by the village. An individual had no right to sell what belonged to the village. Yet soon individuals were trading Wampanoag land for blankets, guns, and liquor.

Metacom met with his people. They decided war was necessary to protect their people, land, and way of life. So, Metacom joined with neighboring tribes to drive out the colonists. Today, this effort is known as King Philip's War. It lasted from 1675 to 1676.

Chief Metacom

The colonists killed Metacom in 1676, and the war ended shortly afterward. The war killed many native people. Several tribes were nearly wiped out. After this, European settlers were able to move west with less resistance.

The Wampanoag Today

Today, many Wampanoag still live within their traditional homelands in New England. Bands such as the Seaconke Wampanoag are fighting to regain their **culture**, traditions, and land.

The Wampanoag Tribe of Gay Head is a **federally recognized** nation. It has about 900 enrolled members. The reservation is located at Aquinnah, on Martha's Vineyard in Massachusetts. They refer to themselves as Aquinnah Wampanoag.

Another large Wampanoag band is the Mashpee Wampanoag. Their community is located on Cape Cod, which is in Massachusetts. Today, the Mashpee are seeking federal recognition and the return of their traditional homelands.

Glenn Marshall is president of the Mashpee Wampanoag Tribal Council.

In 1999, the remains of 17 Wampanoag were found at a construction site in Mashpee. In 2002, the Wampanoag held a ceremony to rebury them. The people will make the site a memorial.

Today, the Wampanoag still hold seasonal ceremonies to give thanks. In August, the Wampanoag hold a Moshup festival. During the Moshup festival, the people dance, sing, and tell stories.

In October, the Wampanoag celebrate Cranberry Day. In the old days, the cranberry ceremony lasted for a number of days. Today, people gather for a day of food, stories, and other **cultural** activities.

In the past, some people have mistakenly thought the Wampanoag were extinct. The Wampanoag want others to know that they still exist. They also want others to know about the importance of the Wampanoag in American history.

Erin Saulnier (left) braids Melanie Roderick's hair as Roderick sews a pair of men's deerskin leggings at Plimoth Plantation in Plymouth, Massachusetts.

Glossary

breechcloth - a piece of hide or cloth, usually worn by men, that wraps between the legs and ties with a belt around the waist.

burl - a hard, rounded woody growth on a tree.

coil method - clay rolled into long ropes that are laid on top of each other in coils to make a pot.

confederacy - a group of people joined together for a common purpose.

consensus - an agreement reached by people in a group.

culture - the customs, arts, and tools of a nation or people at a certain time.

epidemic - the rapid spread of a disease among many people.

federal recognition - the U.S. government's recognition of a tribe as being an independent nation. The tribe is then eligible for special funding and for protection of its reservation lands.

fire - to heat pottery to make it stronger.

game - wild animals hunted for food or sport.

geometric - made up of straight lines, circles, and other simple shapes.

immunity - protection against disease.

leggings - coverings for the legs, usually made of cloth or leather.

ritual - a form or order to a ceremony.

sachem - a North American native chief.

sinew - a band of tough fibers that joins a muscle to a bone.

Web Sites

To learn more about the Wampanoag, visit ABDO Publishing Company on the World Wide Web at **www.abdopub.com**. Web sites about the Wampanoag are featured on our Book Links page. These links are routinely monitored and updated to provide the most current information available.

Index

A

Atlantic Ocean 4, 8

C

Cape Cod 28
ceremonies 6, 7, 16, 30
chiefs 6, 24, 26
children 18, 19
clay 5, 14, 15
clothing 12, 13, 19
crafts 13, 14, 15

D

diseases 24, 25

E

elders 6, 17
Europeans 24, 25, 26, 27

F

family 16, 17
fishing 8, 16, 18, 22, 24, 25
food 8, 9, 12, 14, 17, 18, 19,
     20

G

gardening 8, 9, 16, 17, 19,
     25
gathering 8, 9, 15, 18

H

homelands 4, 5, 20, 21, 24,
     26, 27, 28
homes 10, 11
hunting 8, 12, 16, 19, 20,
     22, 25

J

jewelry 13

L

language 4, 24, 25

M

Martha's Vineyard 4, 21, 28
Massachuset Indians 4
Massasoit 24, 26
Metacom 26, 27

N

Nantucket Island 4
Narraganset Indians 4
Narragansett Bay 4

Nipmuc Indians 4
North America 4

P

Patuxet Indians 24
Pequot Indians 4
Pilgrims 24, 25, 26
powwaws 6

R

reservations 28

S

Squanto 24, 25
stories 6, 17, 20, 21, 30

T

tobacco 16, 20
tools 8, 9, 10, 12, 14, 16,
     17, 18

V

villages 6, 8, 16, 18, 26

W

Wamsutta 26
war 22, 27
weapons 16, 22